SPECTRUM

Language Arts

Grade K

Published by Spectrum
an imprint of Carson-Dellosa Publishing LLC
Greensboro, NC

Spectrum is an imprint of Carson-Dellosa Publishing.

Printed in the United States of America. All rights reserved. Except as permitted under the United States Copyright Act, no part of this publication may be reproduced or distributed in any form or by any means, or stored in a database or retrieval system, without prior written permission from the publisher, unless otherwise indicated. Spectrum is an imprint of Carson-Dellosa Publishing. © 2011 Carson-Dellosa Publishing.

Send all inquiries to:
Carson-Dellosa Publishing
P.O. Box 35665
Greensboro, NC 27425

Printed in Madison, WI USA

1 2 3 4 5 6 WCR 15 14 13 12 11

ISBN 978-0-7696-8000-2

349108454

Table of Contents Grade K

Table of Contents, continued

Aa Bb Cc Dd

Ee Ff Gg Hh

Ii Jj Kk Ll Mm

Nn Oo Pp Qq

Rr Ss Tt Uu Vv

Ww Xx Yy Zz

Lesson 1.1 ABC Order

Follow the letters in ABC order.

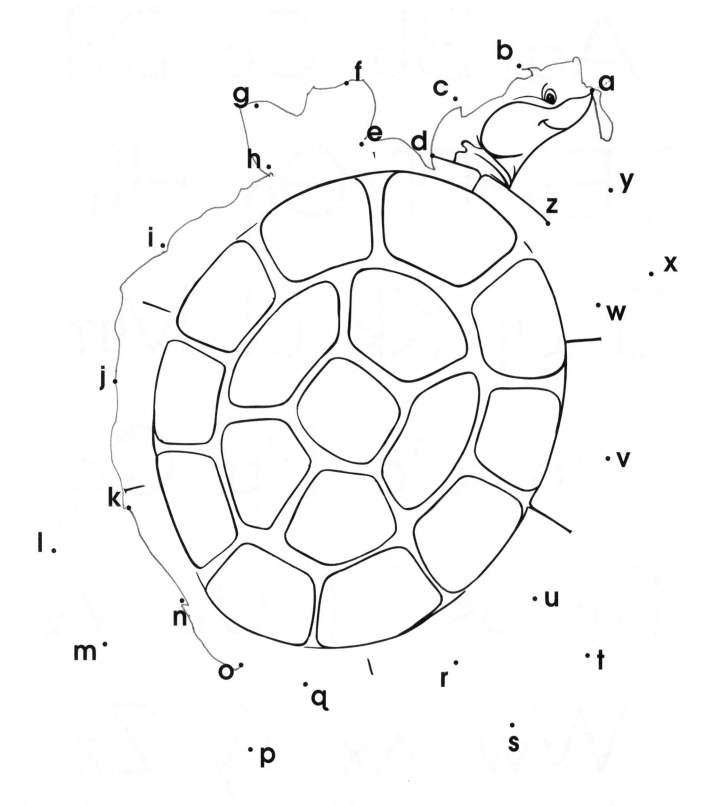

Lesson 1.1 ABC Order

Help the dog find his house. Follow the letters in ABC order.

Lesson 1.2 Capital and Lowercase Letters

Color in each pair of socks that shows a capital and lowercase pair.

Examples: **Vv** **Hh**

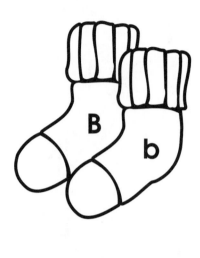

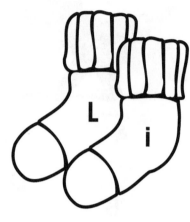

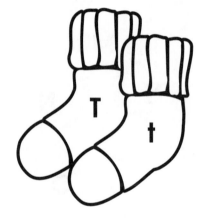

Lesson 1.2 Capital and Lowercase Letters

Write the missing capital letter in each pair. Use the letters in the box.

___ a

___ z

___ d

___ f

Write the missing lowercase letter in each pair. Use the letters in the box.

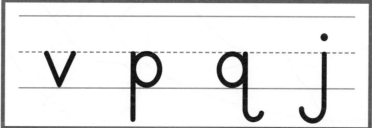

Q ___

V ___

J ___

P ___

Lesson 1.2 Capital and Lowercase Letters

Draw a line to match each capital and lowercase letter.

Lesson 1.2 Capital and Lowercase Letters

Circle the capital letters in the picture. Cross out the lowercase letters.

Lesson 1.3 Letter Recognition

Name each picture. Circle the letter it starts with. Write the letter on the line.

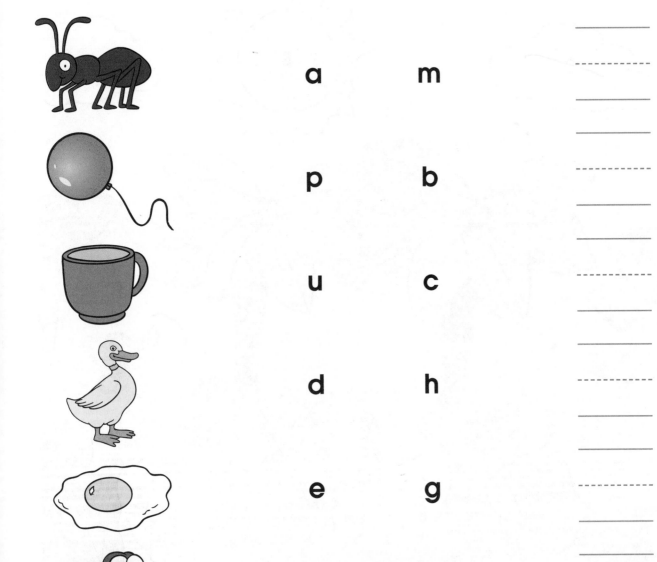

a	m
p	b
u	c
d	h
e	g
s	f
g	s

Lesson 1.3 Letter Recognition

Draw a line from each word to the letter it starts with.

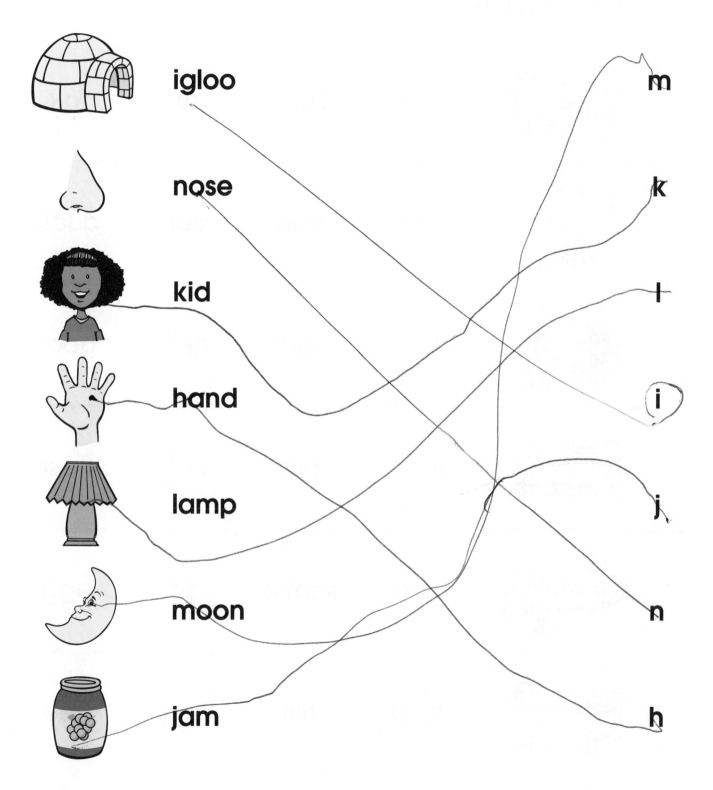

igloo

nose

kid

hand

lamp

moon

jam

m

k

l

i

j

n

h

Lesson 1.3 Letter Recognition

Name each picture. Circle the words in each row that start with the same letter as the picture.

 on   bug   ox   fox

 pie   pan   bee   duck

 jam   gum   quilt   goat

 rake   pig   ring   nest

 zoo   snake   sit   egg

 tiger   hill   lamp   tree

Lesson 1.3 Letter Recognition

Say each picture name. Find the missing letter in the box. Write it on the line.

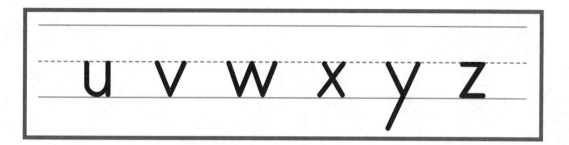

u v w x y z

_____ mbrella

_____ ase

_____ ing

fo _____

_____ o-yo

_____ ebra

Review

Color the fish with capital letters yellow. Color the fish with lowercase letters green.

Review

Name each picture. Circle the letter it starts with. Write the letter on the line.

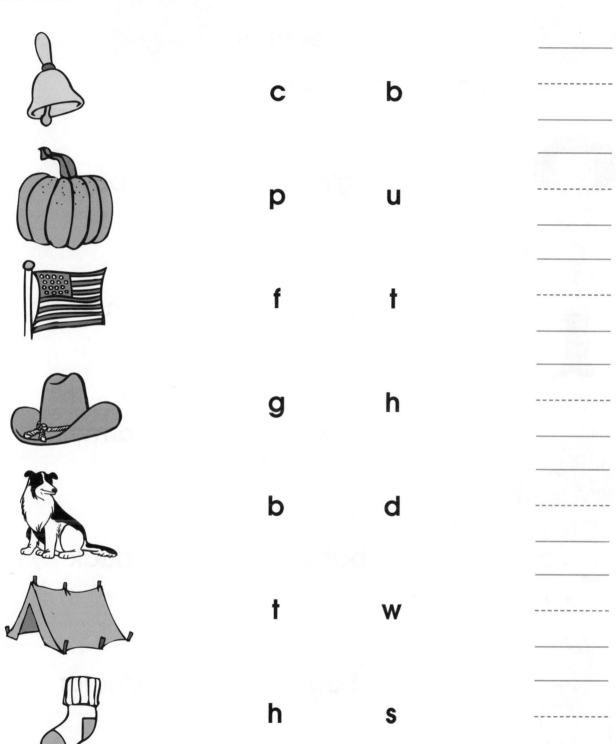

🔔	c	b	_____
🎃	p	u	_____
🏳	f	t	_____
🤠	g	h	_____
🐕	b	d	_____
⛺	t	w	_____
🧦	h	s	_____

NAME _____

Lesson 2.1 Common Nouns

A **noun** is a naming word. It can name a person.

boy

teacher

Circle the noun that names each person.

girl   boy

pan   man

fox   farmer

baby   duck

bug   doctor

Lesson 2.1 Common Nouns

Nouns can name things.

car

ball

Fill in the missing letters in the nouns that name things. Use the words in the box to help you.

chair	desk	book	apple	pen	bag

ba___   bo___k   ap___

___

des___

___

pe___

___hair

Lesson 2.1   Common Nouns

Nouns can also name places.

park    **farm**

Trace the name of each noun that names a place. Write it on the line. Then, color the picture.

   house   _____

   library   _____

   beach   _____

   school   _____

Lesson 2.1 Common Nouns

Remember, **nouns** are naming words. They can name a person, place, or thing.

Look at each picture below and the noun that names it.

Circle the nouns that name a person.

  (farmer)

Make a line under nouns that name a place.

  beach

Cross out nouns that name a thing.

  ~~hat~~

 **baby**

 **bug**

 **boy**

 **store**

 **city**

truck

 **ball**

 **park**

 **woman**

Lesson 2.2 Proper Nouns

A **proper noun** can name a certain person. Proper nouns start with capital letters.

Example: **Mom   Grandma   Ann   Luis**

Trace the names of the people in this family. Circle the capital letter in each name.

Grandpa

Mom   Dad

Jack   Sam   Kate

Lesson 2.2 Proper Nouns

Each person below has two names. Circle the name that is a proper noun. Make a line under the name that is a common noun.

Example: (Harry) <u>clown</u>

Li   doctor

brother   Ben

man   Grandpa

Mom   woman

Lesson 2.2 Proper Nouns

A **proper noun** can also name an animal. Remember, proper nouns start with capital letters.

The horses are missing their names. Choose a name for each horse from the box. Write it on the line. Circle the capital letter.

| Star | Ace | Tom | Rosy | Buck |

Lesson 2.2 Proper Nouns

Circle the name that is a proper noun. Make a line under the name that is a common noun.

Example: (**Max**) <u>**snake**</u>

dog   **Buddy**

Duke   **bird**

Bubbles   **fish**

cat   **Daisy**

Chip   **hamster**

Review

Look at each picture and word below. If the noun names a person, write **P** on the line. If it names a thing, write **T**.

firefighter _____

brush _____

fan _____

girl _____

baby _____

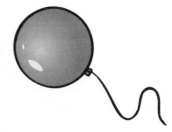

balloon _____

Review

Draw a picture of your family. If you have a pet, draw its picture, too. Write the name of each person and pet on the lines. Ask an adult if you need help spelling the names.

Lesson 2.3 Verbs

A **verb** is an action word. It tells what happens in a sentence.

Examples: **jump**   **eat**   **throw**

Name the action words below. Write the missing letters on the lines.
Use the words in the box to help you.

swim   run   kick   laugh   clap

_____ augh

kic _____

ru _____

cla _____

_____ wim

Lesson 2.3 Verbs

Dad and Ana are cooking. Circle the action word in each sentence that tells what they do.

Dad chops.

Ana mixes.

Ana stirs.

Ana washes.

Dad peels.

They bake.

Lesson 2.3 Verbs

Look at each word and picture. Circle the words that are verbs, or action words.

bus

roll

bend

dress

jump

whale

Lesson 2.3 Verbs

Trace the name of each verb. Write it on the line. Then, color the pictures.

dig

plant

bloom

pick

rake

grow

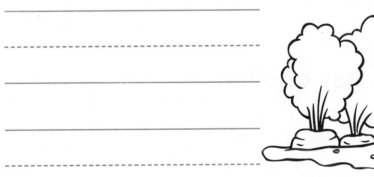

Lesson 2.4 Pronouns

A **pronoun** can take the place of a person's name. **You**, **he**, **she**, **they**, and **it** are pronouns.

Example: Will is six.   (He) is six.

Circle the pronoun in each sentence.
Write it on the line.

He can draw.

She likes to paint.

It is messy and fun.

They make art.

You can color.

Lesson 2.4 Pronouns

Circle the pronoun to complete each sentence. Use the pictures to help you.

He	**She**	**paints with red.**
He	**It**	**likes green.**
She	**They**	**spill the paint!**
It	**They**	**is on the table.**
He	**It**	**wipes it.**
They	**She**	**helps, too.**

Review

Look at each word and picture. Circle the words that are verbs, or action words.

cup

hug

eat

dig

clap

flag

frog

Review

Match each pronoun to the person or thing it names.

it

she

he

they

Write two sentences of your own. Use one pronoun from the pronoun box. Use one verb from the verb box.

Pronouns		
He	**She**	**It**

Verbs		
runs	**skates**	**flies**

_____

- -

_____ .

_____

- -

_____ .

Lesson 2.5 Sentences

A **sentence** is a group of words. It tells a complete thought. A sentence starts with a capital letter. It ends with a period.

Examples: **My name is Ling.** **It is hot.** **I like dogs.**

Look at each sentence. Circle the capital letter. Circle the period.

It is dark.

Look at the stars.

A cat is by the tree.

There are no clouds.

I see the moon.

I hear an owl.

I jump into bed.

Lesson 2.5   Sentences

Name each picture. Then, finish the sentence. Use the words in the box.

Soup	eyes	baby	Dad	read	swim

My mom likes to _____.

My sister is still a _____.

_____ is a good cook.

We all like to _____.

Mom and I have brown _____.

_____ is our favorite dinner.

Lesson 2.5 Sentences

Make a line under each group of words that is a sentence.
Remember, a **sentence** is a complete thought. It starts with a capital
letter. It ends with a period.

a big day

Nico is five.

Lin gives him a new book.

Cal brings a toy car.

eats some cake

likes balloons

Abby and Lex play a game.

Lesson 2.5 Sentences

Look at each group of words. If it is a sentence, make a check mark ✔
on the line. Circle the capital letter. Circle the period.

Sam likes trees. _____

is his tree house _____

Sam reads in it. _____

He plays, too. _____

It has a door. _____

peeks out the windows _____

Lesson 2.6 Statements

A **statement** is a kind of sentence. A statement is a telling sentence. It starts with a capital letter. It ends with a period.

Look at each picture. Trace the statement. Circle the capital letter and the period. Write the statement on the line.

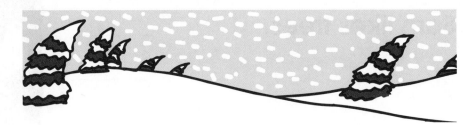

The snow is cold.

_____

_____

I like autumn.

_____

_____

Lesson 2.6 Statements

Look at each picture. Circle the capital letter and the period in the statement. Write another telling sentence about the picture. Ask an adult to help you.

The girl is wet.

Sam has hot feet.

Lesson 2.7 Questions

A **question** is a type of sentence. It is an asking sentence. It starts with a capital letter. It ends with a question mark.

Trace the question marks.

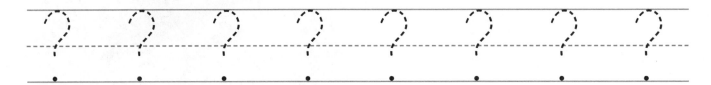

Make a question mark at the end of each question.

What is your name _____

How old are you _____

Do you have a sister or brother _____

What color do you like best _____

Do you have a pet _____

Lesson 2.7 Questions

Make a line under the question in each pair. Circle the question mark.

I draw cars and trucks.  Can you draw?

Do you dance?  I love to dance.

Do you like to play ball?  I play kickball.

I sing funny songs.  What can you sing?

Do you swim?  I swim at the pool.

Review

Each sentence is missing something. Use the box next to each sentence to complete it.

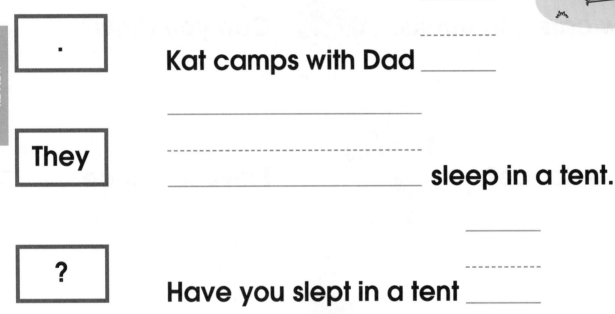

.	Kat camps with Dad _____

They	_____ sleep in a tent.

?	Have you slept in a tent _____

Dad	_____ makes a fire.

.	They cook dinner _____

?	What did they make _____

Review

Look at each sentence below. If it is a **statement**, write **S** on the line. If it is a **question**, write **Q** on the line.

_____   **We go to the park.**

_____   **We can swing.**

_____   **Is there a slide?**

_____   **Can we feed the ducks?**

_____   **I have a snack.**

_____   **Do you like apples?**

Lesson 3.1　Capitalizing the First Word in a Sentence

A **sentence** always starts with a capital letter.

Examples:

Ⓜeg is five.　　Ⓣhe dog is black.　　Ⓣoss me the ball.

Circle the capital letter that starts each sentence.

Jen and Ty make a kite.

They need paper.

Ty picks blue and red.

He cuts the paper.

Where is the glue?

Jen ties the string.

Lesson 3.1 Capitalizing the First Word in a Sentence

Each sentence should start with a capital. Write the word in the box on the line. Use a capital letter.

| it | _____ is a windy day. |

| a | _____ dog runs past. |

| he | _____ tugs on the string. |

| the | _____ kite takes off. |

| jen | _____ calls the dog. |

| he | _____ runs. |

| what | _____ a day to fly a kite! |

Lesson 3.2 Capitalizing the Pronoun I

The word **I** is always spelled with a capital letter. It can start a sentence. It can be in the middle of a sentence.

Circle the word **I** each time you see it.

I like to hike.

My dad and I hike a lot.

Dad has our bag.

I help him pack it.

We walk for awhile.

Then, I ask Dad for a snack.

Dad and I love the woods.

Lesson 3.2 Capitalizing the Pronoun I

The word **I** is missing from each sentence.
Write a capital **I** on each line.

_____
_ _ _ _ _ _ _ _

_____ like to look for animals.

_____
_ _ _ _ _ _ _

Dad and _____ saw a deer once.

_____
_ _ _ _ _ _ _ _

_____ see birds a lot.

_____
_ _ _ _ _ _ _

Dad and _____ want to see a possum.

_____
_ _ _ _ _ _ _

Will _____ see a fox one day?

_____
_ _ _ _ _ _ _

_____ hope so!

Lesson 3.3 Capitalizing Names

Names start with a capital letter.

Examples: (T)ess   (W)ill   (M)in

Write your name on the line. Ask an adult if you need help.

_____

- -

_____

None of the names below start with a capital.
Write each name on the line. Use a capital letter.

dante _____   **erik** _____

tom _____   **may** _____

cam _____   **jess** _____

rico _____   **nora** _____

NAME _____

Lesson 3.3 Capitalizing Names

The **names of pets** start with a capital letter, too.

Examples: uddy ulu (S)ocks

Each pet needs a name. Choose a name from the box. Write it under the pet. Use a capital letter.

| lady   sam   spot   jake   gus   bella   coco |

Review

Look at each sentence. Write the word in the box on the line. Use a capital letter.

dogs

_____
_____ can bark.

the

_____
_____ owl hoots.

i

Lee and _____ hear the cat purr.

birds

_____
_____ chirp in the tree.

cows

_____
_____ say moo.

i

_____ hear bees buzz.

Review

Circle each letter that should be a capital.

Min

Jon

jane

amad

lex

Ava

ben

lucky

rocky

Luna

star

bo

Daisy

Lesson 3.4 Periods

A **period** comes at the end of a sentence. It shows you where the sentence ends.

Example: My cat's name is Laney.

Circle the period in each sentence.

The sky is blue.

Roses are red.

The dove is gray.

Worms are brown.

The crow is black.

Grass is green.

Lesson 3.4 Periods

Add a period to each sentence.

Ben likes blue balloons _____

Pat's pig is pink _____

Rosy has a red wagon _____

Greg has a green bag _____

Bess has black hair _____

Yuri's jacket is yellow _____

Lesson 3.5 Question Marks

A **question mark** comes at the end of a question. It shows you where the question ends.

Examples: Did you see the frog(?)   Is that Tim's bus(?)

Circle each question mark.

Who wants nuts?

Is the soup hot?

Can we fry the eggs?

Will Jon eat grapes?

Did you make rice?

Did you drop that peach?

Lesson 3.5 Question Marks

Write a question mark at the end of each question.

_____

Do you like corn _____

_____

Where is the jam _____

_____

What is for lunch _____

_____

Can we have peas _____

_____

Are we out of milk _____

_____

What is a kiwi _____

Review

Draw a line under the question in each pair. Circle the question mark.

Fox and Pig have a race.   Who will win?

Cat is asleep.   Will Mouse wake him?

Where is Duck?   She is at the pond.

Why is Frog sad?   He lost his lily pad.

Cow looks for Sheep.   Is she in the barn?

Review

Look at each sentence. If it has a **P**, write a period at the end. If it has a **Q**, write a question mark.

P   **We went to the beach** _____

P   **The waves are big** _____

Q   **Did you see the fish** _____

P   **I have a beach ball** _____

Q   **Is the sand hot** _____

Q   **Do you want to swim** _____

Lesson 3.6 Beginning Consonant Sounds

Say each picture name. Circle the letter for the beginning sound.
Write the letter on the line.

g   b   _____

h   t   _____

l   b   _____

w   m   _____

m   d   _____

n   j   _____

Lesson 3.6   Beginning Consonant Sounds

Say each picture name. Draw a line between the words that start with the same sound.

car

doll

van

zebra

fence

rug

pie

vase

pig

ring

fox

zipper

cat

duck

Lesson 3.6 Beginning Consonant Sounds

Say the name of each picture. Fill in the missing letter for each word.
Choose from the letters in the box.

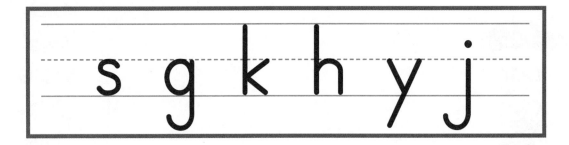

_____ oat

_____ arn

_____ ey

_____ eep

_____ un

_____ orse

Lesson 3.6 Beginning Consonant Sounds

Color the pictures in each row with the same beginning sound. Write the letter for the sound.

   _____

  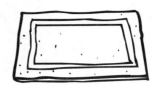 _____

  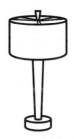 _____

   _____

   _____

Lesson 3.7   Ending Consonant Sounds

Circle the pictures in each row with the same ending sound. Write the letter for the sound.

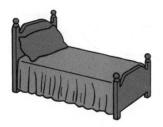  

Lesson 3.7 Ending Consonant Sounds

Say the name of each picture. Match the pictures that end with the same sound.

fox

bird

box

pin

spoon

hill

crab

bus

web

Lesson 3.7 Ending Consonant Sounds

Circle the words in each row that end with /p/, like **stamp**.

| ship | tub | cap | bed |

Circle the words in each row that end with /s/, like **grass**.

| buzz | dress | bus | ax |

Circle the words in each row that end with /m/, like **broom**.

| pan | drum | gum | sun |

Lesson 3.7 Ending Consonant Sounds

Say the name of each picture. Fill in the missing letter for each word.
Choose from the letters in the box.

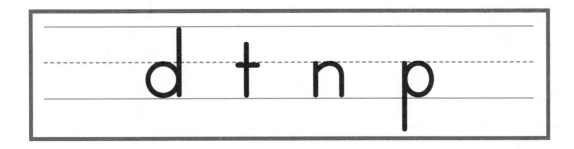

shee___

li___

ma___

lam___

ne___

sle___

Review

Color the pictures in each row that start with the same sound. Write the letter for the sound.

_____
- - - - - - -
_____

_____
- - - - - - -
_____

_____
- - - - - - -
_____

_____
- - - - - - -
_____

 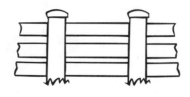 

_____
- - - - - - -
_____

Review

Say each picture name. Circle the letter for the ending sound. Write the letter on the line.

s   d

_____
- - - - - - -
_____

n   p

_____
- - - - - - -
_____

h   t

_____
- - - - - - -
_____

l   g

_____
- - - - - - -
_____

x   w

_____
- - - - - - -
_____

REVIEW

Lesson 3.8 Short Vowel Sounds

Short **a** makes the vowel sound you hear in **cap** .

Say the name of each picture. Circle the pictures that have the short **a** sound, like **pan**  .

Lesson 3.8   Short Vowel Sounds

Short **e** makes the vowel sound you hear in **pen** .

Say the name of each picture. Fill in the missing letter for each word.

   w __ b

   b __ d

   h __ n

   n __ st

10   t __ n

Lesson 3.8 Short Vowel Sounds

Short **i** makes the vowel sound you hear in **crib** .

Help the fish find its pond. Follow the words that have the short **i** sound, like in **wig** .

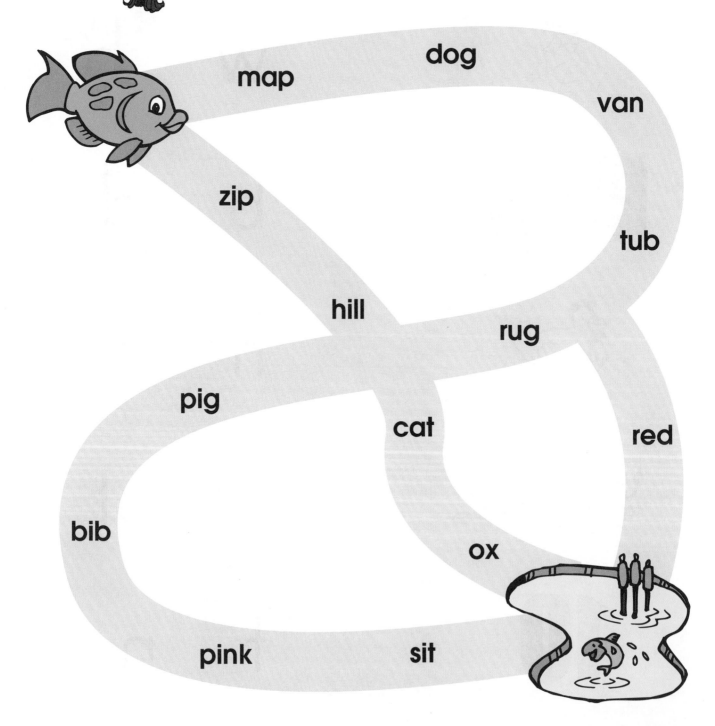

Lesson 3.8 Short Vowel Sounds

Short **o** makes the vowel sound you hear in **log** .

Short **u** makes the vowel sound you hear in **brush** .

Say each picture name. Circle the vowel sound you hear in each word.

pot		o	u
tub		o	u
box		o	u
bus		o	u
drum		o	u
dog		o	u

Review

Color the fish with short **o** words green. Color the fish with short **i** words blue.

Review

Say the name of each picture. Match the pictures that have the same vowel sound.

flag

cat

bib

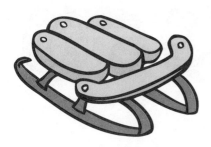

sled

ring

bed

truck

rope

bus

Chapter 4 Usage

Lesson 4.1 Plurals with **s**

Plural means **more than one**. Make a word plural by adding **s**.

Example: 1 sock    4 sock**s**

Draw a line to match each word to the correct picture.

   **cars**

   **truck**

   **plane**

   **boats**

Lesson 4.1 Plurals with **s**

Look at each picture and word. If there is more than one of something, add **s**.

 hat _____

 dress _____

 sock _____

 coat _____

 skirt _____

 boot _____

Lesson 4.2 Rhyming Words

Words that **rhyme** sound alike. The middle and ending sound is the same.

Examples: pig   wig

box    fox

Name the first picture. Circle the words in each row that rhyme with it.

mop   **hat**   **bat**

map   **bed**   **red**

rock   **top**   **drum**

Lesson 4.2 Rhyming Words

Draw a line between the rhyming picture names.

nail

house

truck

spoon

moon

pail

mouse

duck

Lesson 4.2 Rhyming Words

Fill in the missing letters for each pair of rhymes.

 pan    m _____

 frog    d _____

 pig    w _____

 flag    b _____

Lesson 4.2 Rhyming Words

Say each picture name. In the box, draw a picture of a rhyming word.

3

Review

Help the cat find her party hat. Follow the words that rhyme through the maze.

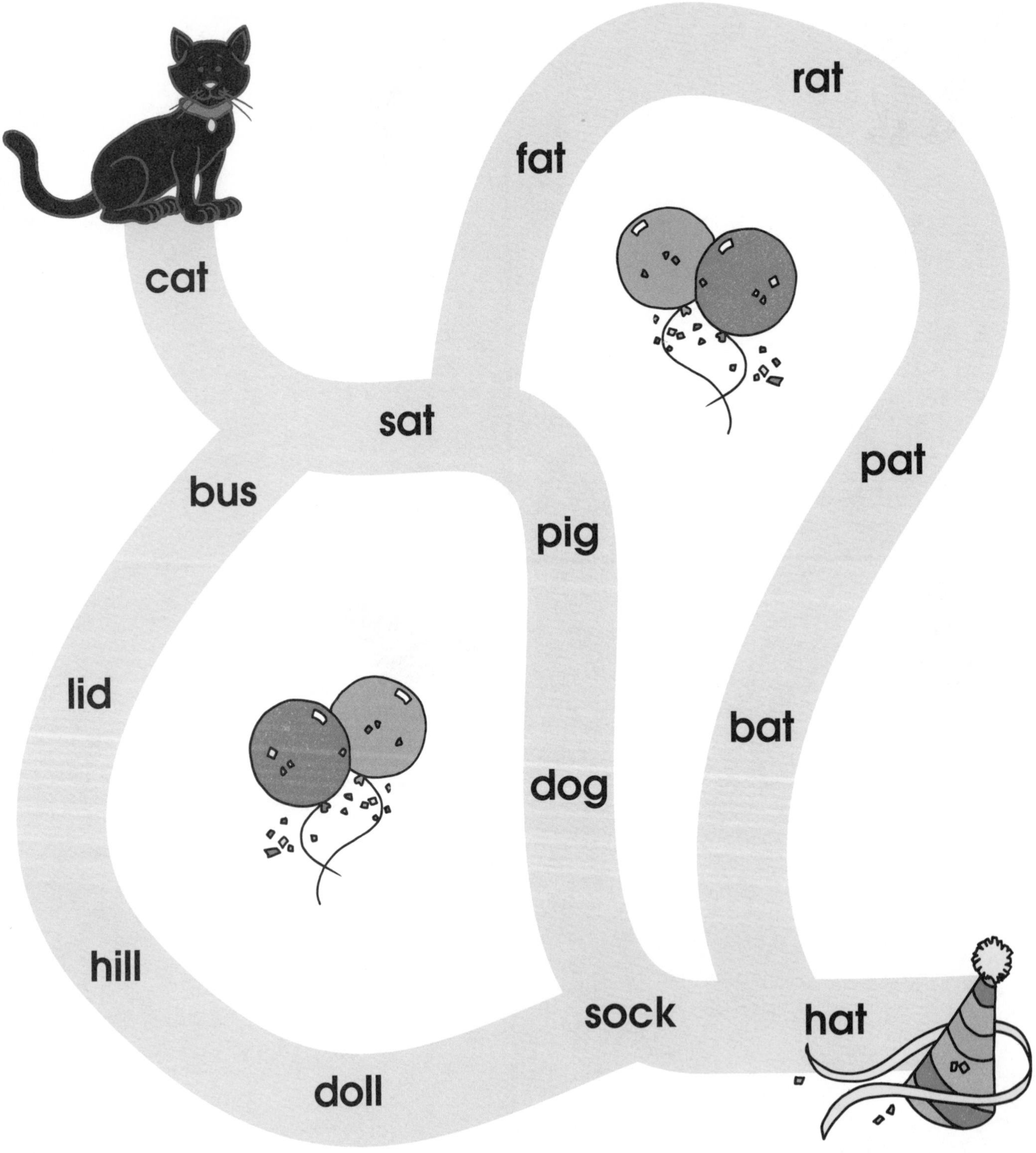

rat

fat

cat

sat

bus

pig

pat

lid

bat

dog

hill

sock   hat

doll

Review

Finish each rhyme. Use the words in the box.

| bug | bib | bat | tree | frog |

_____

a bee _____

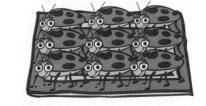

_____

a _____ rug

_____

a _____ hat

_____

a _____ log

_____

a crib _____

Lesson 4.3   Order Words

Some words tell in what order things happen. **First**, **next**, and **last** are order words.

first   **next**   **last**

Trace each word. Then, write it on your own.

 first _____

 next _____

 last _____

Lesson 4.3 Order Words

Before and **after** are also order words.

before

after

Look at each **before** picture. Draw a picture of what might happen **after**.

Before	**After**

Lesson 4.4   Sequencing

Trace each number. Then, write it on your own.

1 = = = 2 = = = = 3 = = = = 4 = = = =

Look at each picture. Which happened first? Which happened last?
Show the order. Write **1**, **2**, **3**, or **4** under each picture.

_____

- - - - - - -

_____

_____

- - - - - - -

_____

_____

- - - - - - -

_____

_____

- - - - - - -

_____

Lesson 4.4 Sequencing

Look at each picture. Show the order. Write **1**, **2**, **3**, or **4** under each picture.

_____

- - - - - - - - - -

_____

_____

- - - - - - - - - -

_____

_____

- - - - - - - - - -

_____

_____

- - - - - - - - - -

_____

Lesson 4.4 Sequencing

What do you think happens **after** the dog's bath? Draw a picture in the box.

Lesson 4.4 Sequencing

The pictures below are in order. One is missing. What do you think happens in that picture? Draw it.

1

2

3

4

Review

Look at the pictures. Show the order. Write **first**, **next**, and **last** under them.

_____

- -

_____

_____

- -

_____

_____

- -

_____

Review

The pictures below are in order. One is missing. What do you think happens in that picture? Draw it.

1

2

3

4

Lesson 4.5 Antonyms

Antonyms are opposites.

up   **down**

big   **small**

Draw a line to match each picture to its antonym.

full

winter

day

right

summer

empty

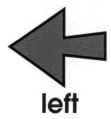
left

night

Lesson 4.5 Antonyms

Draw a line to match each word to its antonym.

 sad

wet

happy

hot

little

big

full

down

up

Lesson 4.5 Antonyms

Look at each antonym pair. Fill in the missing letters. Use the words in the box to help you.

stop	open	tall	in

 short    t _ ll

 o _____    closed

 go    ___op

 i___    out

Lesson 4.5 Antonyms

Name each picture. Trace its antonym.

happy  said

white  black

back 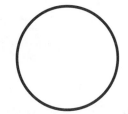 front

down  up

night  day

Lesson 4.6   Category Words

Words that are like each other can be put in a group.

Foods: apple **, bread** **, soup** **, pizza**

Make a circle around the animal words. Make a line under things you find in a house.

lamp

dog

fish

frog

bed

cat

couch

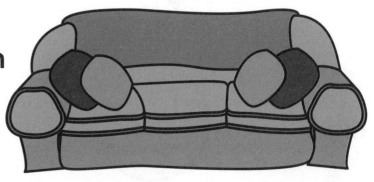

Lesson 4.6 Category Words

Draw a line from each word to the group it belongs in.

School Words

Outside Words

desk

grass

crayon

bird

tree

book

Review

Draw a line to match each picture to its antonym.

cold

left

big

full

down

right

empty

up

hot

little

Review

Look at each group. Cross out the things that do not belong.

 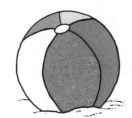  

Lesson 5.1   Telling What You Know

You can write to share what you know.

**Cats have fur. They have tails.
They sleep a lot. Cats like milk.**

Make a list of three things you know about. You can use the ideas in the box. You can use your own ideas, too.

soccer   dog   baby

train   art   frog

Lesson 5.2 Using Telling Words to Describe

Telling words make your writing more fun to read. Telling words let others know how something looks or feels.

Examples: a **black** dog   **hot** soup   a **small** mouse

Pick a word from the box that tells more about the picture. Write the word on the line.

| pink   blue |  | a _____ **dress** |

| soft   brown |  | a _____ **puppy** |

| big   green |  | a _____ **tree** |

| red   long |  | _____ **hair** |

Lesson 5.3 Proofreading

When you write, check your work. Look for mistakes.

If a period is missing, add it like this: **Dan has a dog**⊙

If a letter should be a capital, fix it like this: **i am hot.**

Fix the mistake in each sentence. Use the marks you learned.

we like to sled.

We run up the hill

Mira can go fast

she has a red hat.

Tom's nose is cold

will we get more snow?

Lesson 5.4　Revising

First, find your mistakes. Then, fix them.

M̲y̲ ball is green⊙　**My ball is green.**

Fix the mistakes in each sentence.
Write it on the line.

max is a boy

_____

- -

_____

lulu is his cat

_____

- -

_____

she has white fur

_____

- -

_____

Lesson 5.5 Writing a Friendly Letter

Writing a letter is a good way to keep in touch. You can tell a story. You can share some news.

> Write the date in the right corner.

January 18, 2011

> Start with **Dear** and the person's name. Use capital letters.

Dear Grandpa,

> You can ask a question.

How are you? Is it hot in Tampa?

> Share some news.

It is very cold here. I like the snow. We got two feet last week! Mom and I cut out snowflakes. We hung them up.

I miss you. Come visit soon!

> A closing can be words like **Love**, **Yours Truly**, or **Your Friend**.

Love,

> Sign your name. Remember to start it with a capital letter.

Carlos

Lesson 5.5 Writing a Friendly Letter

Write your own letter. Ask an adult to help you.

_____

- -

Dear _____ **,**

_____

- -

_____

- -

_____

- -

_____

- -

_____

- -

Yours Truly,

_____

- -

_____

Follow the letters in ABC order.

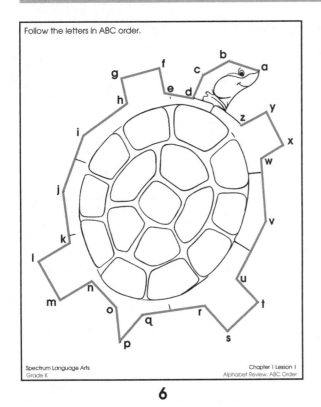

Help the dog find his house. Follow the letters in ABC order.

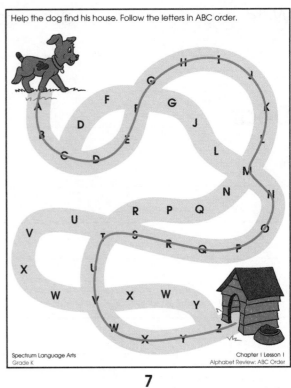

Color in each pair of socks that shows a capital and lowercase pair.

Examples: **Vv** **Hh**

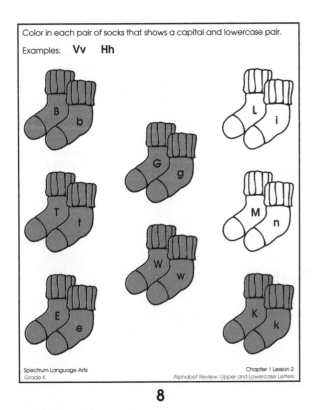

Write the missing capital letter in each pair. Use the letters in the box.

Write the missing lowercase letter in each pair. Use the letters in the box.

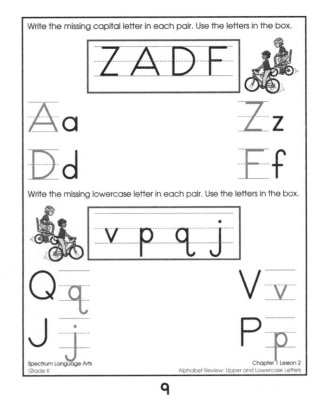

Answer Key

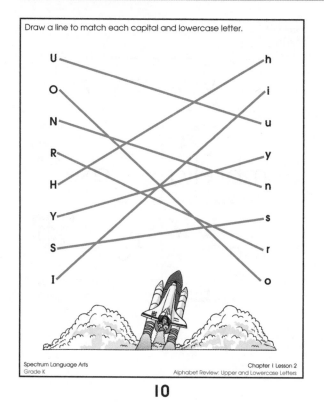

Draw a line to match each capital and lowercase letter.

U	h
O	i
N	u
R	y
H	n
Y	s
S	r
I	o

Spectrum Language Arts
Grade K

Chapter 1 Lesson 2
Alphabet Review: Upper and Lowercase Letters

10

Circle the capital letters in the picture. Cross out the lowercase letters.

Spectrum Language Arts
Grade K

Chapter 1 Lesson 2
Alphabet Review: Upper and Lowercase Letters

11

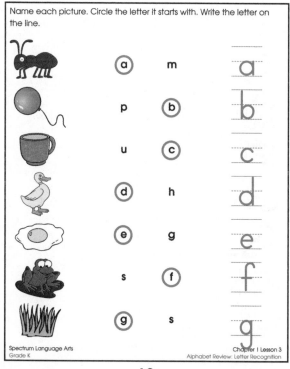

Name each picture. Circle the letter it starts with. Write the letter on the line.

(a) m   a

p (b)   b

u (c)   c

(d) h   d

(e) g   e

s (f)   f

(g) s   g

Spectrum Language Arts
Grade K

Chapter 1 Lesson 3
Alphabet Review: Letter Recognition

12

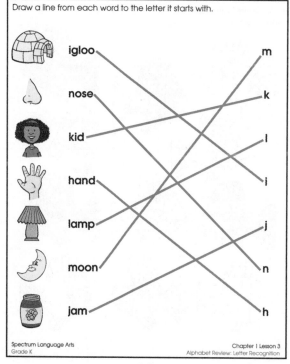

Draw a line from each word to the letter it starts with.

igloo	m
nose	k
kid	l
hand	i
lamp	j
moon	n
jam	h

Spectrum Language Arts
Grade K

Chapter 1 Lesson 3
Alphabet Review: Letter Recognition

13

Spectrum Language Arts
Grade K

Answer Key

Answer Key

Name each picture. Circle the words in each row that start with the same letter as the picture.

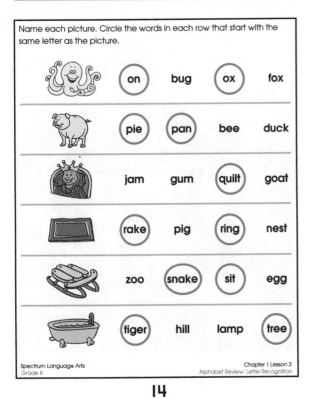

(on)	bug	(ox)	fox
(pie)	(pan)	bee	duck
jam	gum	(quilt)	goat
(rake)	pig	(ring)	nest
zoo	(snake)	(sit)	egg
(tiger)	hill	lamp	(tree)

Spectrum Language Arts
Grade K

Chapter 1 Lesson 3
Alphabet Review: Letter Recognition

14

Say each picture name. Find the missing letter in the box. Write it on the line.

u v w x y z

u mbrella   v ase

w ing   fo x

y o-yo   z ebra

Spectrum Language Arts
Grade K

Chapter 1 Lesson 3
Alphabet Review

15

Color the fish with capital letters yellow. Color the fish with lowercase letters green.

Spectrum Language Arts
Grade K

Review Chapter 1 Lessons 1–3
Alphabet

16

Name each picture. Circle the letter it starts with. Write the letter on the line.

c	(b)	b
(p)	u	p
(f)	t	f
g	(h)	h
b	(d)	d
(t)	w	t
h	(s)	s

Spectrum Language Arts
Grade K

Review Chapter 1 Lessons 1–3
Alphabet

17

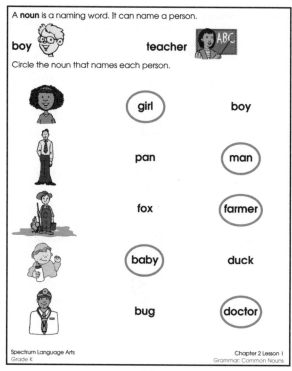

Answer Key

A **proper noun** can name a certain person. Proper nouns start with capital letters.

Example: **Mom   Grandma   Ann   Luis**

Trace the names of the people in this family. Circle the capital letter in each name.

Ⓖrandpa

Ⓜom   Ⓓad

Ⓙack   Ⓢam   Ⓚate

Each person below has two names. Circle the name that is a proper noun. Make a line under the name that is a common noun.

Example: (Harry)   clown

Ⓛi   doctor

brother   (Ben)

man   (Grandpa)

(Mom)   woman

A **proper noun** can also name an animal. Remember, proper nouns start with capital letters.

The horses are missing their names. Choose a name for each horse from the box. Write it on the line. Circle the capital letter.

Star   Ace   Tom   Rosy   Buck

Location of names will vary.

Ⓑuck   Ⓣom

Ⓐce

Ⓡosy   Ⓢtar

Circle the name that is a proper noun. Make a line under the name that is a common noun.

Example: (Max)   snake

dog   (Buddy)

(Duke)   bird

(Bubbles)   fish

cat   (Daisy)

(Chip)   hamster

Look at each picture and word below. If the noun names a person, write **P** on the line. If it names a thing, write **T**.

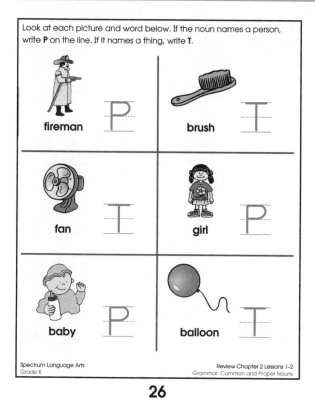

fireman — P

brush — T

fan — T

girl — P

baby — P

balloon — T

Draw a picture of your family. If you have a pet, draw its picture, too. Write the name of each person and pet on the lines. Ask an adult if you need help spelling the names.

Drawings will vary.

Names will vary.

A **verb** is an action word. It tells what happens in a sentence.

Examples: **jump**   **eat**   **throw**

Name the action words below. Write the missing letters on the lines. Use the words in the box to help you.

| swim | run | kick | laugh | clap |

Laugh

kick

run

clap

swim

Dad and Ana are cooking. Circle the action word in each sentence that tells what they do.

Dad (chops)

Ana (mixes.)

Ana (stirs.)

Ana (washes.)

Dad (peels.)

They (bake.)

Look at each word and picture. Circle the words that are verbs, or action words.

Trace the name of each verb. Write it on the line. Then, color the pictures.

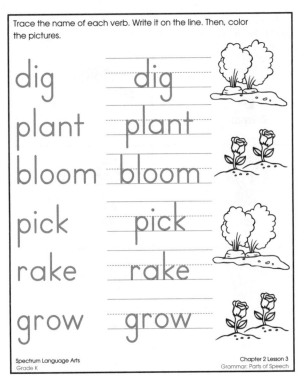

A **pronoun** can take the place of a person's name. **You, he, she, they,** and **it** are pronouns.

Example: Will is six.   He is six.

Circle the pronoun in each sentence. Write it on the line.

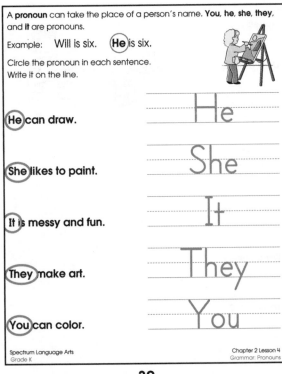

Circle the pronoun to complete each sentence. Use the pictures to help you.

Look at each word and picture. Circle the words that are verbs, or action words.

cup

hug   eat

dig

clap   frog

flag

Spectrum Language Arts
Grade K

Review Chapter 2 Lessons 3-4
Grammar: Verbs and Pronouns

34

Match each pronoun to the person or thing it names.

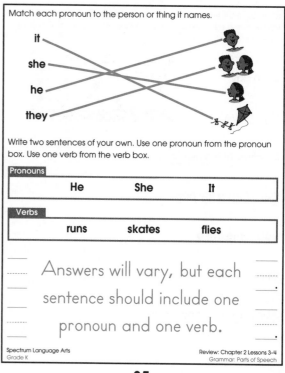

it
she
he
they

Write two sentences of your own. Use one pronoun from the pronoun box. Use one verb from the verb box.

Pronouns		
He	She	It

Verbs		
runs	skates	flies

Answers will vary, but each sentence should include one pronoun and one verb.

Spectrum Language Arts
Grade K

Review: Chapter 2 Lessons 3-4
Grammar: Parts of Speech

35

A **sentence** is a group of words. It tells a complete thought. A sentence starts with a capital letter. It ends with a period.

Examples: **My name is Ling.   It is hot.   I like dogs.**

Look at each sentence. Circle the capital letter. Circle the period.

(I) is dark(.)

(L)ook at the stars(.)

(A) cat is by the tree(.)

(T)here are no clouds(.)

(I) see the moon(.)

(I) hear an owl(.)

(I) jump into bed(.)

Spectrum Language Arts
Grade K

Chapter 2 Lesson 5
Grammar: Sentences

36

Name each picture. Then, finish the sentence. Use the words in the box.

Soup	eyes	baby	Dad	read	swim

My mom likes to ___ swim .

My sister is still a ___ baby .

Dad ___ is a good cook.

We all like to ___ read .

Mom and I have brown ___ eyes .

Soup ___ is our favorite dinner.

Spectrum Language Arts
Grade K

Chapter 2 Lesson 5
Grammar: Sentences

37

Spectrum Language Arts
Grade K

Make a line under each group of words that is a sentence. Remember, a **sentence** is a complete thought. It starts with a capital letter. It ends with a period.

a big day

<u>Nico is five.</u>

<u>Lin gives him a new book.</u>

<u>Cal brings a toy car.</u>

eats some cake

likes balloons

<u>Abby and Lex play a game.</u>

Look at each group of words. If it is a sentence, make a check mark ✔ on the line. Circle the capital letter. Circle the period.

Ⓢam likes tree⊙.   ✔

is his tree house

Ⓢam reads in i⊙.   ✔

Ⓗe plays to⊙.   ✔

Ⓘ has a doo⊙.   ✔

peeks out the windows

A **statement** is a kind of sentence. A statement is a telling sentence. It starts with a capital letter. It ends with a period.

Look at each picture. Trace the statement. Circle the capital letter and the period. Write the statement on the line.

Ⓣhe snow is col⊙
The snow is cold.

Ⓘ like autumn⊙
I like autumn.

Look at each picture. Circle the capital letter and the period in the statement. Write another telling sentence about the picture. Ask an adult to help you.

Ⓣhe girl is wet⊙
Answers will vary.

Ⓢam has hot feet⊙
Answers will vary.

Answer Key

A **question** is a type of sentence. It is an asking sentence. It starts with a capital letter. It ends with a question mark.

Trace the question marks.

? ? ? ? ? ? ?

Make a question mark at the end of each question.

What is your name **?**

How old are you **?**

Do you have a sister or brother **?**

What color do you like best **?**

Do you have a pet **?**

Spectrum Language Arts
Grade K

Chapter 2 Lesson 7
Grammar: Questions

42

Make a line under the question in each pair. Circle the question mark.

I draw cars and trucks. Can you draw**?**

Do you dance**?** I love to dance.

Do you like to play ball**?** I play kickball.

I sing funny songs. What can you sing**?**

Do you swim**?** I swim at the pool.

Spectrum Language Arts
Grade K

Chapter 2 Lesson 7
Grammar: Sentences

43

Each sentence is missing something. Use the box next to each sentence to complete it.

.	Kat camps with Dad **.**
They	They sleep in a tent.
?	Have you slept in a tent **?**
Dad	Dad makes a fire.
.	They cook dinner **.**
?	What did they make **?**

Spectrum Language Arts
Grade K

Review Chapter 2 Lessons 5–7
Grammar: Sentences

44

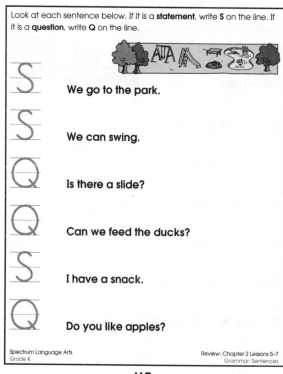

Look at each sentence below. If it is a **statement**, write **S** on the line. If it is a **question**, write **Q** on the line.

S We go to the park.

S We can swing.

Q Is there a slide?

Q Can we feed the ducks?

S I have a snack.

Q Do you like apples?

Spectrum Language Arts
Grade K

Review: Chapter 2 Lessons 5–7
Grammar: Sentences

45

Spectrum Language Arts
Grade K

Answer Key

A **sentence** always starts with a capital letter.

Examples:

Ⓜeg is five.   Ⓣhe dog is black.   Ⓣoss me the ball.

Circle the capital letter that starts each sentence.

Ⓙen and Ty make a kite.

Ⓣhey need paper.

Ⓣy picks blue and red.

Ⓗe cuts the paper.

Ⓦhere is the glue?

Ⓙen ties the string.

Spectrum Language Arts
Grade K

Chapter 3 Lesson 1
Mechanics: Capitalizing the First Word in a Sentence

46

Each sentence should start with a capital. Write the word in the box on the line. Use a capital letter.

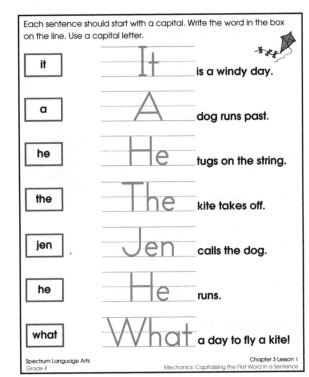

it	It is a windy day.
a	A dog runs past.
he	He tugs on the string.
the	The kite takes off.
jen	Jen calls the dog.
he	He runs.
what	What a day to fly a kite!

Spectrum Language Arts
Grade K

Chapter 3 Lesson 1
Mechanics: Capitalizing the First Word in a Sentence

47

The word **I** is always spelled with a capital letter. It can start a sentence. It can be in the middle of a sentence.

Circle the word **I** each time you see it.

Ⓘ like to hike.

My dad and Ⓘ hike a lot.

Dad has our bag.

Ⓘ help him pack it.

We walk for awhile.

Then, Ⓘ ask Dad for a snack.

Dad and Ⓘ love the woods.

Spectrum Language Arts
Grade K

Chapter 3 Lesson 2
Mechanics: Capitalization

48

The word **I** is missing from each sentence. Write a capital I on each line.

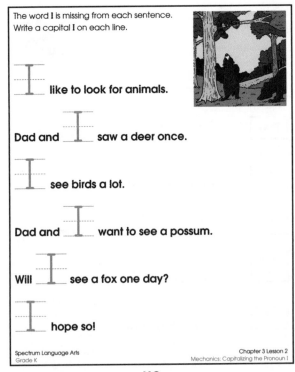

I like to look for animals.

Dad and I saw a deer once.

I see birds a lot.

Dad and I want to see a possum.

Will I see a fox one day?

I hope so!

Spectrum Language Arts
Grade K

Chapter 3 Lesson 2
Mechanics: Capitalizing the Pronoun I

49

Spectrum Language Arts
Grade K

116

Answer Key

Names start with a capital letter.

Examples: (T)ess (W)ill (M)in

Write your name on the line. Ask an adult if you need help.

Answers will vary. The name should begin with a capital letter.

None of the names below start with a capital.
Write each name on the line. Use a capital letter.

dante	Dante	erik	Erik
tom	Tom	may	May
cam	Cam	jess	Jess
rico	Rico	nora	Nora

Spectrum Language Arts
Grade K

Chapter 3 Lesson 3
Mechanics: Capitalizing Names

50

The **names of pets** start with a capital letter, too.

Examples: (B)uddy (L)ulu (S)ocks

Each pet needs a name. Choose a name from the box. Write it under the pet. Use a capital letter.

| lady | sam | spot | jake | gus | bella | coco |

Answers will vary, but each pet's name should begin with a capital letter.

Spectrum Language Arts
Grade K

Chapter 3 Lesson 3
Mechanics: Capitalization

51

Look at each sentence. Write the word in the box on the line. Use a capital letter.

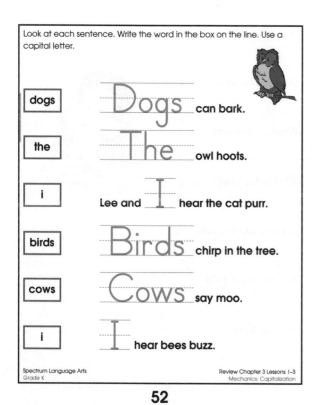

dogs	Dogs can bark.
the	The owl hoots.
i	Lee and I hear the cat purr.
birds	Birds chirp in the tree.
cows	Cows say moo.
i	I hear bees buzz.

Spectrum Language Arts
Grade K

Review Chapter 3 Lessons 1–3
Mechanics: Capitalization

52

Circle each letter that should be a capital.

Min   Jon   (j)ane   (a)mad

(l)ex   Ava   (b)en

(l)ucky   (r)ocky   Luna

(s)tar   (b)o   Daisy

Spectrum Language Arts
Grade K

Review Chapter 3 Lessons 1–3
Mechanics: Capitalization

53

Answer Key

A **period** comes at the end of a sentence. It shows you where the sentence ends.

Example: My cat's name is Laney.

Circle the period in each sentence.

The sky is blue.

Roses are red.

The dove is gray.

Worms are brown.

The crow is black.

Grass is green.

Add a period to each sentence.

Ben likes blue balloons.

Pat's pig is pink.

Rosy has a red wagon.

Greg has a green bag.

Bess has black hair.

Yuri's jacket is yellow.

A **question mark** comes at the end of a question. It shows you where the question ends.

Examples: Did you see the frog?   Is that Tim's bus?

Circle each question mark.

Who wants nuts?

Is the soup hot?

Can we fry the eggs?

Will Jon eat grapes?

Did you make rice?

Did you drop that peach?

Write a question mark at the end of each question.

Do you like corn?

Where is the jam?

What is for lunch?

Can we have peas?

Are we out of milk?

What is a kiwi?

Answer Key

Write a line under the question in each pair. Circle the question mark.

Fox and Pig have a race. <u>Who will win**?**</u>

Cat is asleep. <u>Will Mouse wake him**?**</u>

<u>Where is Duck**?**</u> She is at the pond.

<u>Why is Frog sad**?**</u> He lost his lily pad.

Cow looks for Sheep. <u>Is she in the barn**?**</u>

Look at each sentence. If it has a **P**, write a period at the end. If it has a **Q**, write a question mark.

P We went to the beach **.**

P The waves are big **.**

Q Did you see the fish **?**

P I have a beach ball **.**

Q Is the sand hot **?**

Q Do you want to swim **?**

Say each picture name. Circle the letter for the beginning sound. Write the letter on the line.

g   **b**   b

h   **t**   t

l   b   l

w   m   w

m   d   m

n   j   n

Say each picture name. Draw a line between the words that start with the same sound.

car — cat
doll — duck
van — vase
zebra — zipper
fence — fox
rug — ring
pie — pig

Answer Key

Say the name of each picture. Fill in the missing letter for each word. Choose from the letters in the box.

s g k h y j

g oat   y arn

k ey   j eep

s nake   h orse

Spectrum Language Arts
Grade K
Chapter 3 Lesson 6
Mechanics: Beginning Consonant Sounds

62

Color the pictures in each row with the same beginning sound. Write the letter for the sound.

s

w

r

l

b

Spectrum Language Arts
Grade K
Chapter 3 Lesson 6
Mechanics: Beginning Consonant Sounds

63

Circle the pictures in each row with the same ending sound. Write the letter for the sound.

d

t

g

Spectrum Language Arts
Grade K
Chapter 3 Lesson 7
Mechanics: Ending Consonant Sounds

64

Say the name of each picture. Match the pictures that end with the same sound.

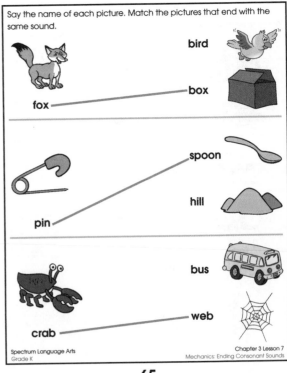

bird

fox ———— box

spoon

hill

pin

bus

web

crab

Spectrum Language Arts
Grade K
Chapter 3 Lesson 7
Mechanics: Ending Consonant Sounds

65

Answer Key

Circle the words in each row that end with /p/, like **stamp**.

ship   tub   cap   bed

Circle the words in each row that end with /s/, like **grass**.

buzz   dress   bus   ax

Circle the words in each row that end with /m/, like **broom**.

pan   drum   gum   sun

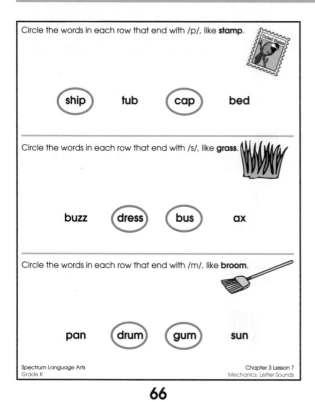

Spectrum Language Arts
Grade K

Chapter 3 Lesson 7
Mechanics: Letter Sounds

66

Say the name of each picture. Fill in the missing letter for each word. Choose from the letters in the box.

d t n p

shee**p**   li**d**

ma**n**   lam**p**

ne**t**   sle**d**

Spectrum Language Arts
Grade K

Chapter 3 Lesson 7
Mechanics: Ending Consonant Sounds

67

Color the pictures in each row that start with the same sound. Write the letter for the sound.

h

b

m

s

f

Spectrum Language Arts
Grade K

Review Chapter 3 Lessons 6–7
Mechanics: Consonant Sounds

68

Say each picture name. Circle the letter for the ending sound. Write the letter on the line.

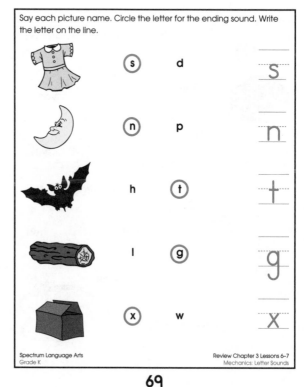

s   d   s

n   p   n

h   t   t

l   g   g

x   w   x

Spectrum Language Arts
Grade K

Review Chapter 3 Lessons 6–7
Mechanics: Letter Sounds

69

Spectrum Language Arts
Grade K

Answer Key

Answer Key

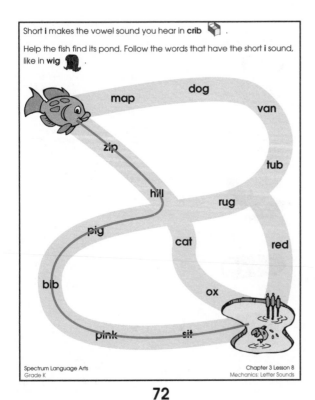

Short **e** makes the vowel sound you hear in **pen**.

Say the name of each picture. Fill in the missing letter for each word.

w e b

b e d

h e n

n e st

t e n

Spectrum Language Arts
Grade K

Chapter 3 Lesson 8
Mechanics: Short Vowel Sounds

71

Short **o** makes the vowel sound you hear in **log**.

Short **u** makes the vowel sound you hear in **brush**.

Say each picture name. Circle the vowel sound you hear in each word.

pot — **o** u

tub — o **u**

box — **o** u

bus — o **u**

drum — o **u**

dog — **o** u

Spectrum Language Arts
Grade K

Chapter 3 Lesson 8
Mechanics: Short Vowel Sounds

73

Spectrum Language Arts
Grade K

Answer Key

Answer Key

Color the fish with short **o** words green. Color the fish with short **i** words blue.

Spectrum Language Arts
Grade K

Review Chapter 3 Lesson 8
Mechanics: Short Vowel Sounds

74

Say the name of each picture. Match the pictures that have the same vowel sound.

flag — cat

ring

sled — bed

truck — bus

Spectrum Language Arts
Grade K

Review Chapter 3 Lesson 8
Mechanics: Short Vowel Sounds

75

Plural means **more than one**. Make a word plural by adding **s**.

Example: 1 sock   4 sock**s**

Draw a line to match each word to the correct picture.

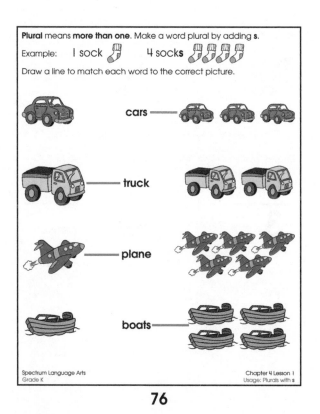

cars

truck

plane

boats

Spectrum Language Arts
Grade K

Chapter 4 Lesson 1
Usage: Plurals with **s**

76

Look at each picture and word. If there is more than one of something, add **s**.

hat s

dress

sock s

coat s

skirt

boot s

Spectrum Language Arts
Grade K

Chapter 4 Lesson 1
Usage: Plurals with **s**

77

Answer Key

Words that **rhyme** sound alike. The middle and ending sound is the same.

Examples: pig   wig
            box   fox

Name the first picture. Circle the words in each row that rhyme with it.

	mop	(hat)	(bat)
	map	(bed)	(red)
	(rock)	top	drum

Spectrum Language Arts
Grade K

Chapter 4 Lesson 2
Usage

78

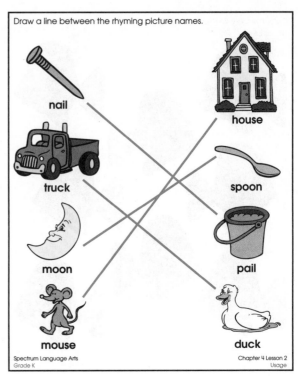

Draw a line between the rhyming picture names.

nail

house

truck

spoon

moon

pail

mouse

duck

Spectrum Language Arts
Grade K

Chapter 4 Lesson 2
Usage

79

Fill in the missing letters for each pair of rhymes.

pan   m an

frog   d og

pig   w ig

flag   b ag

Spectrum Language Arts
Grade K

Chapter 4 Lesson 2
Usage: Rhyming Words

80

Say each picture name. In the box, draw a picture of a rhyming word.

Possible answer: a picture of a box

Possible answer: a picture of a cake

— Answers will vary. —

3

Possible answer: a picture of a bee

Possible answer: a picture of a cat

Spectrum Language Arts
Grade K

Chapter 4 Lesson 2
Usage: Rhyming Words

81

Answer Key

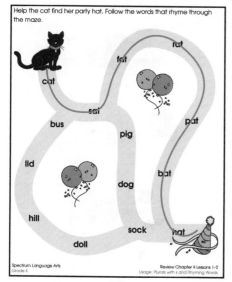

82

83

84

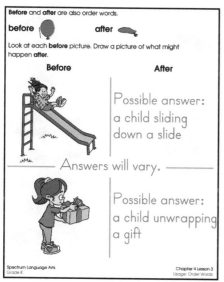

85

86

87

Answer Key

What do you think happens **after** the dog's bath? Draw a picture in the box.

Answers will vary.

Possible answer: a picture of a dog shaking itself

Spectrum Language Arts
Grade K

Chapter 4 Lesson 4
Usage: Sequencing

88

The pictures below are in order. One is missing. What do you think happens in that picture? Draw it.

Answers will vary.

Possible answer: a small plant

Spectrum Language Arts
Grade K

Chapter 4 Lesson 4
Usage: Sequencing

89

Look at the pictures. Show the order. Write **first**, **next**, and **last** under them.

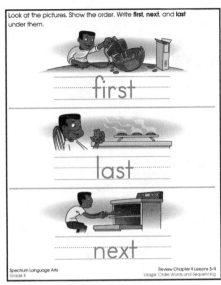

first

last

next

Spectrum Language Arts
Grade K

Review Chapter 4 Lessons 3-4
Usage: Order Words and Sequencing

90

The pictures below are in order. One is missing. What do you think happens in that picture? Draw it.

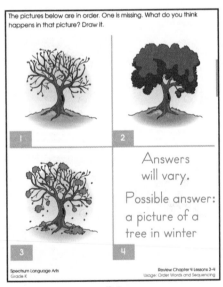

Answers will vary.

Possible answer: a picture of a tree in winter

Spectrum Language Arts
Grade K

Review Chapter 4 Lessons 3-4
Usage: Order Words and Sequencing

91

Antonyms are opposites.

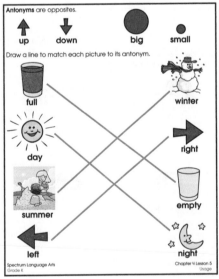

Draw a line to match each picture to its antonym.

full
day
summer

winter
right
empty
night

Spectrum Language Arts
Grade K

Chapter 4 Lesson 5
Usage

92

Draw a line to match each word to its antonym.

happy — sad
wet

big — hot
little

up — full
down

Spectrum Language Arts
Grade K

Chapter 4 Lesson 5
Usage: Antonyms

93

Answer Key

Look at each antonym pair. Fill in the missing letters. Use the words in the box to help you.

stop	open	tall	in

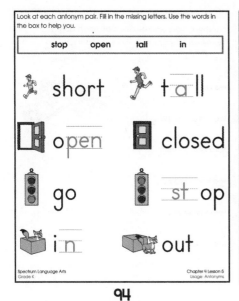

short — ta ll

op en — closed

go — st op

i n — out

Spectrum Language Arts
Grade K

Chapter 4 Lesson 5
Usage: Antonyms

94

Name each picture. Trace its antonym.

happy — sad

white — black

back — front

down — up

night — day

Spectrum Language Arts
Grade K

Chapter 4 Lesson 5
Usage: Antonyms

95

Words that are like each other can be put in a group.

Foods: apple , bread , soup , pizza

Make a circle around the animal words. Make a line under things you find in a house.

lamp   dog   fish

frog   bed

cat   couch

Spectrum Language Arts
Grade K

Chapter 4 Lesson 6
Usage: Category Words

96

Draw a line from each word to the group it belongs in.

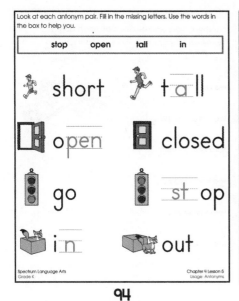

School Words   Outside Words

desk   grass

crayon   bird

tree   book

Spectrum Language Arts
Grade K

Chapter 4 Lesson 6
Usage: Category Words

97

Draw a line to match each picture to its antonym.

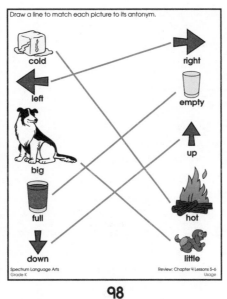

cold   right

left   empty

big   up

full   hot

down   little

Spectrum Language Arts
Grade K

Review: Chapter 4 Lessons 5-6
Usage

98

Look at each group. Cross out the things that do not belong.

Spectrum Language Arts
Grade K

Review Chapter 4 Lessons 5-6
Usage: Antonyms and Category Words

99

Spectrum Language Arts
Grade K

Answer Key

You can write to share what you know.

**Cats have fur. They have tails.
They sleep a lot. Cats like milk.**

Make a list of three things you know about. You can use the ideas in the box. You can think of your own, too.

soccer	dog	baby
train	art	frog

———— Answers will vary. ————

Spectrum Language Arts
Grade K

Chapter 5 Lesson 1
Writer's Guide: Telling What You Know

100

Telling words make your writing more fun to read. Telling words let others know how something looks or feels.

Examples: a **black** dog   **hot** soup   a **small** mouse

Pick a word from the box that tells more about the picture. Write the word on the line.

Answers will vary.

pink blue	a _____ dress
soft brown	a _____ puppy
big green	a _____ tree
red long	_____ hair

Spectrum Language Arts
Grade K

Chapter 5 Lesson 2
Writer's Guide: Using Telling Words to Describe

101

When you write, check your work. Look for mistakes.

If a period is missing, add it like this: **Dan has a dog**⊙

If a letter should be a capital, fix it like this: i am hot.

Fix the mistake in each sentence. Use the marks you learned.

W
we like to sled.

We run up the hill⊙

Mira can go fast⊙

S
she has a red hat.

Tom's nose is cold⊙

W
will we get more snow?

Spectrum Language Arts
Grade K

Chapter 5 Lesson 3
Writer's Guide

102

First, find your mistakes. Then, fix them.

M
my ball is green⊙   My ball is green.

Fix the mistakes in each sentence.
Write it on the line.

M
max is a boy⊙

Max is a boy.

L
lulu is his cat⊙

Lulu is his cat.

S
she has white fur⊙

She has white fur.

Spectrum Language Arts
Grade K

Chapter 5 Lesson 4
Writer's Guide

103

Write your own letter. Ask an adult to help you.

Dear _____ ,

Letters will vary.
They should include capital
letters and periods.

Yours Truly,

Spectrum Language Arts
Grade K

Chapter 5 Lesson 5
Writer's Guide: Writing a Friendly Letter

105
